Cool-Doo Math

[GRADE 1 AND 2]

www.cool-doo.com

04

Andrew Feng

First Printing: 2015

ISBN: 978-0-9938371-3-5

www.cool-doo.com

Jack

Cool-Doo

Sleepy-Doo

To know the adventure of Jack and his gang,
please read *TUM* - The Unmoved Mover.
www.t-u-m.net

Dr. Green

Dr. Z

Jr. Z

To know the adventure of Jack and his gang,
please read *TUM* - The Unmoved Mover.
www.t-u-m.net

Contents

Removing TUM CHiPS

ANSWER

SOLUTION

Jack's board has 4 rows and
4 columns. Since each row and
column only have one chip,
there are only 4 chips needed to
be left on the board.

Altogether, there are 11 chips
on the board now, so 11 - 4 = 7,
which is the number of chips
needed to be removed.

The correct answer is B.

How Many Pillows?

Cool-Doo and Sleepy-Doo are comparing each other's pillows.

Altogether we have 54 pillows.
How many pillows does Cool-Doo have?
Hmff...

ANSWER

SOLUTION

If subtracting 50 pillows from the total 54 pillows, there are only 4 pillows left, and now Cool-Doo and Sleepy-Doo have the same number of pillows.

So, Cool-Doo has 2 pillows, which is half of 4 pillows.

The correct answer is C.

Building a TUM Land

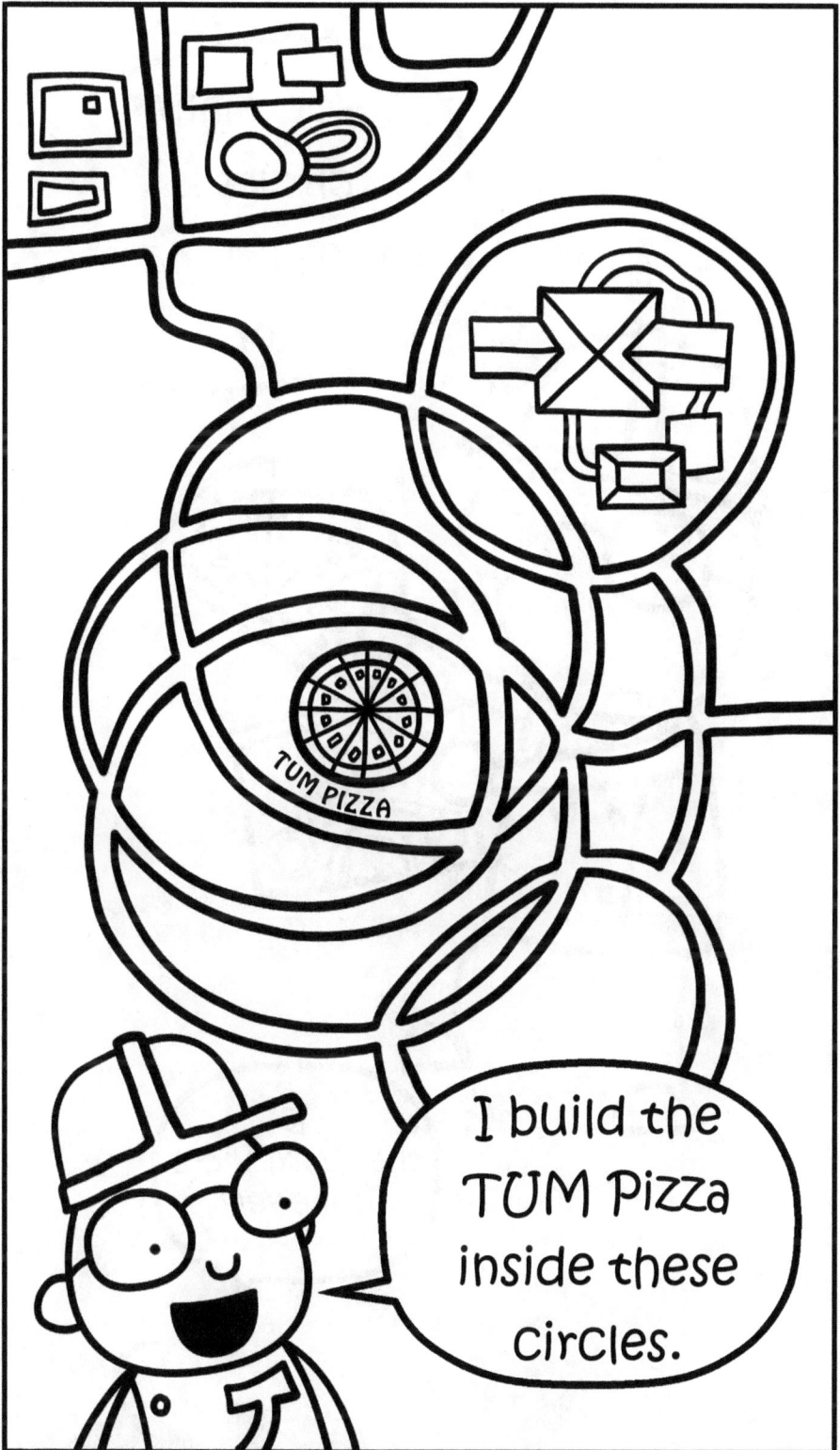

I build the TUM Pizza inside these circles.

ANSWER

SOLUTION

All you have to do is to count the number of circles the TUM Pizza is in.

However, watch out for the overlapping circles. Count carefully!

The correct answer is D.

Pod Racing

Jack and Cool-Doo were choosing their space pods for a race.

Each pod had its own colour.

I want that one!

No, I want that one!

The blue pod is in front of pod #4, but behind pod #1.

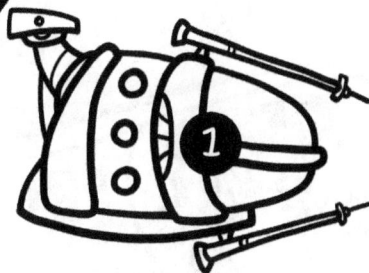

The red pod is behind the blue pod.

The green pod is in front of the blue pod, but it is not the 1st pod.

The black pod is behind the blue pod.

The black pod is in front of the red pod.

Which pod is the red one?

ANSWER

SOLUTION

For this question, you have to follow the instructions.

The blue pod must be either Pod 2 or Pod 3, since it is between Pod 1 and Pod 4.

The green pod is not the first one, but it is in front of the blue pod. That means the green pod must be Pod 2 and the blue pod is Pod 3.

Behind the blue pod, there are only 2 pods left. Since the black pod and the red pod are both behind the blue one, and the black one is in front of the red one, the red pod must be Pod 5.

The correct answer is D.

How Many Pages?

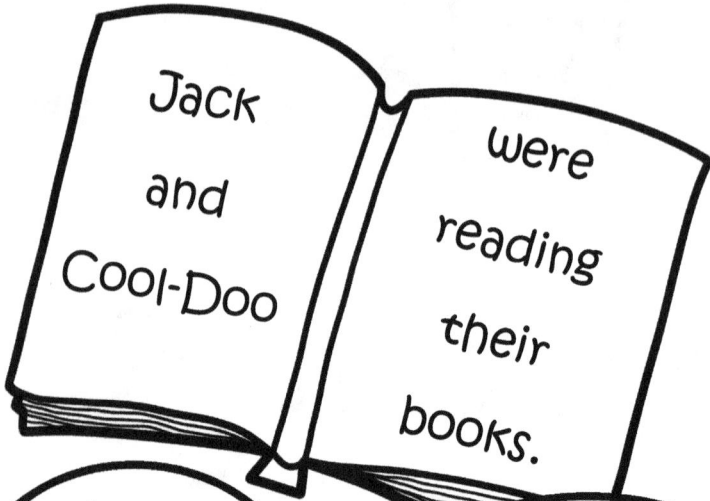

Jack and Cool-Doo were reading their books.

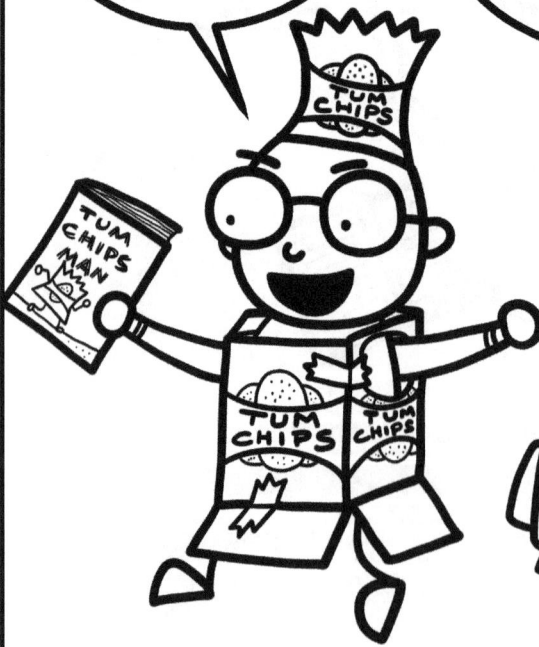

Beat him, TUM Chips Man!

I guess costumes aren't so bad after all.

So far I read all the pages before page 51.

So far I read all the pages before page 40.

I'm wondering what's the sum of the pages we have read and who is faster?

I think I read much faster than that Jack does.

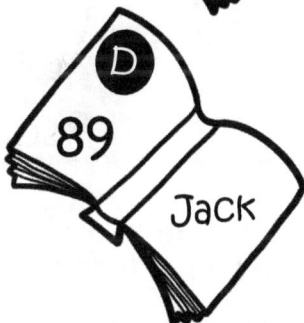

ANSWER

SOLUTION

Jack reads all the pages before page 51, so he reads 50 pages.

Cool-Doo reads all the pages before page 40, so he reads 39 pages.

Altogether, they read 50 + 39 = 89 pages.

Apparently, Jack reads more pages.

The correct answer is D.

.T.U.M.
The Unmoved Mover

ANDREW FENG

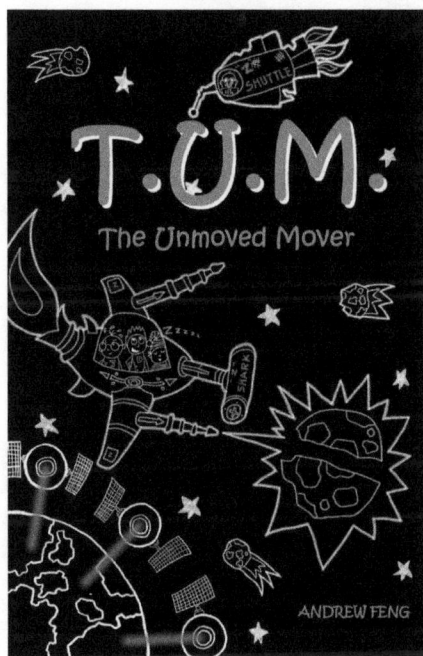

Do you get along with your brother?

Jack doesn't!

Although he has always expected to have a brother to play with, he finds his dream of brotherhood shattered after he gets a really "special" one. This special one always impresses Jack's parents. Plus, this special one also has a special friend of his own, and things always stir up crazily.

Finally, a chance comes for Jack to impress his parents. His hometown is placed in danger while he and the other two special guys are in a space camp, and he only has one night left to become the hero. But, of course, his "special" brother also wants to be the hero.

The clock is ticking...can they make it? And which one will make it?

(www.t-u-m.net)

> ❝ *A **lively** adventure that **charms** and **delights!**❞*
>
> ## - KIRKUS REVIEWS

About the Author

"Myths can be true; fairy tales can be true; even lies can be true. So, why not my dream?"

Who made up this quote?

Andrew Feng did!

He was born on a snowy day.

He loves to draw, to read, and enjoys playing Ping Pong and video games.

He wants to be an awesome-ordinary guy.

www.ingramcontent.com/pod-product-compliance
Lightning Source LLC
Chambersburg PA
CBHW060545030426
42337CB00021B/4442